On the Front Cover

The cover image is a photo of the Clarence depot on the West Shore Railroad in the Hollow. The depot stood on the south side of the tracks just east of Salt Road. The West Shore Railroad purchased all the depot buildings as identical prefabricated units and then dropped them off at various locations along the line. Images of the Pembroke and Bowmansville depots look exactly like this one of station in the Hollow.

This book has been made possible through a bequest of the Berry Estate

Clarence Historical Society Press would like to thank Mr. Gordon Berry for his donation to the Historical Society of the Town of Clarence, which has made this book possible. We are indebted to his kindness, and we hope this book justifies his faith in us.

<u>*Dedication:*</u>

This book is dedicated to my niece, Josephine Kohler. Your father loves Rhode Island, but this book will help you to know his roots.

Clarence: Images of The Hollow

Copyright © 2005 by C. Douglas Kohler
ISBN 0-9765085-0-8

First Published 2005 by Clarence Historical Society Press

Library of Congress Catalog Number 2005900809

Printed by Dual Printing
340 Nagel Drive
Cheektowaga, NY 14225

Clarence Schools

The building on the left was Parker Academy. The rear four windows are from the original school that is pictured on the previous page. The northern section, added in 1897, included a bell tower visible on the left and an observatory. The new Parker High School is visible in the background. The Academy was demolished in 1924, and Parker High School was torn down in 1980.

Table of Contents

Acknowledgements:

On the eve of our bicentennial, what better way to understand where we are today than to look into our past? Clarence has experienced unprecedented growth over the last thirty years. As we have grown in population, we are losing those people who remember our town as it was in the early decades of the 1900's. In compiling this series, we have gone to the "old timers" for their recollections about Clarence from the 1920's on. Their stories have been invaluable, and we hope that you will enjoy their perspectives on how our town has changed and grown. They have given generously of their time, and we have enjoyed each moment spent reminiscing.

Additionally, this book has been a true team effort. May Coppola, who is the epitome of a genealogist in our eyes, Rachel Plaisted, and Clarence Historical Museum curator Alicia Braaten have been instrumental and patient in finding images that appear in this book. Barbara Gilmour has arranged innumerable meetings with people willing to share their remembrances of our town. Town Supervisor, Kathleen Hallock, Town Historian, Mark Woodward, and the trustees of the Historical Society of the Town of Clarence have been unflagging in their support.

Thanks are due to Rose Synor for creating the "Clarence font" at the top of each page. She rendered it from the handwritten address on the postcard image featured on the cover. Thank you also to Elizabeth Dunne for help with some last minute photographic issues, and to Chris DiGaudio from the Clarence Central Schools for copies of the school board minutes from the 1940's. Several people have contributed to our knowledge of the Liberty Diner: Dan Zilka and the American Diner Museum shared a copy of the Liberty Diner brochure; Mike Engle supplied information about the company in the 1930's, and Rob Schofield of Mazia's Pizzeria shared images of his original Liberty Diner.

~

Preface:

There are many ways to write a history book and even more ways to organize it. I wanted this one to be as easy to use as possible. I hope that the reader can pick it up and navigate through it intuitively, so it is written as if you were driving down Main Street. The book is laid out from west to east with slight detours down Shisler Road or Ransom Road until you get to Newstead. Then, imagine that you head back west along Greiner Road until you return to where you started.

The process of writing a new history book for the Town of Clarence began in the summer of 2002. As the trustees of the Historical Society of the Town of Clarence looked toward the forthcoming bicentennial, it occurred to many of us that Oneta and Diane Baker's *History of the Town of Clarence* was almost 20 years old. Throughout that summer we met with publishers and grant writers; we discussed what we would like to see in a new book and whether we could produce it ourselves. In the end, we decided to wait until our Genealogy Department relocated to the Gerber Library that Mr. Wilson Greatbatch had purchased and then donated to the Town of Clarence.

By June 2004, the Genealogy Building was far enough along for me to access the treasures housed there. In doing research for this book, I came across blueprints for the original Buffalo Truck, survey plans for the Masonic Club, journals of the Reverend Glezen Fillmore and photographs, some of which appear here and others that did not fit the format of book but that were fascinating in their own right. Then there are the family stories. I have been captivated by the family names that constantly reappear: Schurr, Dietz, Long, Muchow, Lapp, Shope, Strickler and so many others. They are the silken threads from which our town's history is woven.

After looking through the *Road Books* compiled by Isabella Stage, Oneta Baker and Lillian Ebersole, I decided to let the pictures tell the story. Luckily, photographers at the turn of the century had exquisite equipment, and the pictures are startling in their clarity.

The stories I have compiled barely scratch the surface. In some cases, there are no pictures available. For instance, people are always asking about the lake on the east side of Shisler Road. It is an old quarry that the West Shore Railroad operated, but no one ever thought to take a picture of it. Viola Monkelbaan remembers the children of the Hollow sledding down Academy Street across Main Street and out onto Salt Road. There are tanneries and stores, grand homes and buildings long gone. There are too many stories to tell here, but I hope that you enjoy reading this book as much as I have enjoyed preparing it.

Of course, a work like this does not get done without the help of many. I extend my thanks to David Brace, Alicia Braaten, May Coppola, Barbara Gilmour, Colleen Johnson and Rachel Plaisted who provided historical feedback. My thanks also to Jennie Rook, Carrie Duggan and my father, Charles Kohler, who were my sentinels of grammar and syntax, and to Jerome Neuner, who gave it one last "going over." Any remaining errors or omissions are solely my own.

Finally, I could not have done this without the love and support of my parents, Charles and Nancy, who engendered my love of history; my brother Greg who cheerfully fixed any and all computer issues with grace and aplomb; my sister-in-law Donna who proofread the final draft, my grandmother Charlotte who provided unwavering support and encouragement; and, of course, my wife Charlotte who read, proofed, listened, critiqued and tolerated long, long absences while I was ensconced in the museum for hours and hours on end. I can never thank all of you enough.

C. Douglas Kohler
Clarence Center, NY
December 2004

Southeastern Clarence

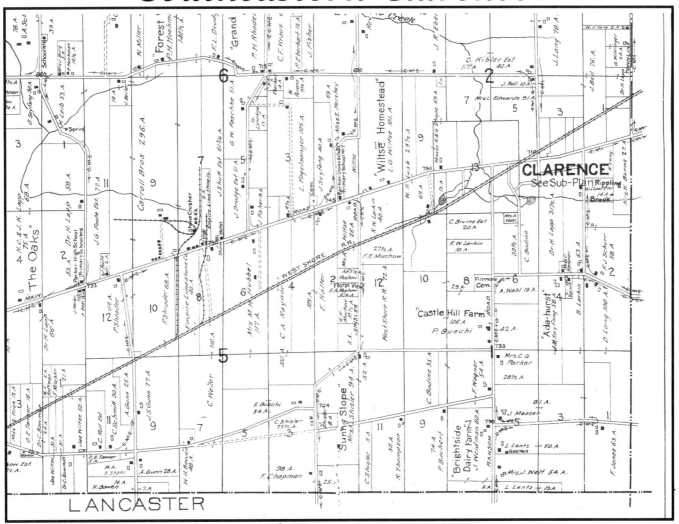

circa 1909

Clarence Hollow

The Hollow

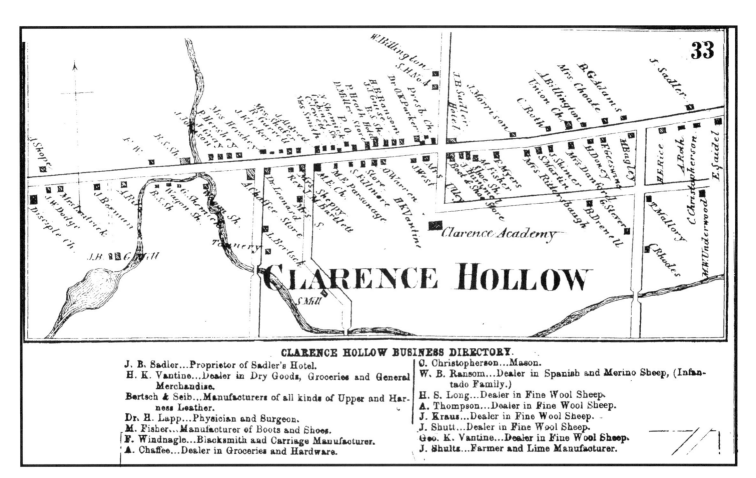

33

CLARENCE HOLLOW BUSINESS DIRECTORY.

J. B. Sadler...Proprietor of Sadler's Hotel.

H. K. Vantine...Dealer in Dry Goods, Groceries and General Merchandise.

Bertsch & Seib...Manufacturers of all kinds of Upper and Harness Leather.

Dr. H. Lapp...Physician and Surgeon.

M. Fisher...Manufacturer of Boots and Shoes.

F. Windnagle...Blacksmith and Carriage Manufacturer.

A. Chaffee...Dealer in Groceries and Hardware.

C. Christopherson...Mason.

W. B. Ransom...Dealer in Spanish and Merino Sheep, (Infantado Family.)

H. S. Long...Dealer in Fine Wool Sheep.

A. Thompson...Dealer in Fine Wool Sheep.

J. Kraus...Dealer in Fine Wool Sheep.

J. Shutt...Dealer in Fine Wool Sheep.

Geo. K. Vantine...Dealer in Fine Wool Sheep.

J. Shults...Farmer and Lime Manufacturer.

circa 1880

12

JOSEPH ELLICOTT

Joseph Ellicott & The Holland Land Company

In 1797, fifty-two leaders of the Seneca Nation of the Iroquois Confederacy signed the Treaty of Big Tree ceding their lands to the Holland Land Company. Actually a consortium of six Dutch banking houses, the Holland Land Company promptly appointed Theophilus Cazenove as their General Agent. He, in turn, chose Joseph Ellicott as his chief surveyor. In 1798, Ellicott began the "Great Survey," dividing the Holland Land Purchase into six-mile wide ranges that extended from the Pennsylvania border to the shores of Lake Ontario. Townships were then measured off running from east to west again in six-mile intervals.

13

Joseph Ellicott & The Holland Land Company

Joseph Ellicott laid out two major north-south transit lines in order to map the Holland Land Purchase. Transit Road still traverses what was once the West Transit Line. In late 1799, Paul Busti replaced Cazenove as General Agent. With the completion of the Great Survey, Busti appointed Ellicott as chief land agent. By 1799, Busti was concerned about the lack of development and authorized Ellicott to find six "reputable individuals" to open lodgings for travelers headed west. For their efforts, each tavern owner would receive between fifty and 150 acres of land "at liberal time for payment, without interest, at the lowest price the Company will sell their lands." On 1 September 1799, Asa Ransom took possession of 150 acres of land in Clarence Hollow.

Gunnville

Like the Looneyville station in Alden, the Gunnville depot was a relatively small stop along the West Shore Railroad. The platform was located north of Jefferson Gunn's homestead on the east side of Gunnville Road. Gunn had purchased a portion of Lot #5 from the Holland Land Company, which included a limekiln on the property. Limekilns were very common in the southern part of town where "the Ledge," an escarpment of Onondaga limestone, provided a ready supply of stone. Jefferson Gunn died in 1893 but was survived by his wife, Caroline Gunn, pictured above.

The Proposed

JUNIOR - SENIOR HIGH SCHOOL

CLARENCE CENTRAL SCHOOL BOARD

Clarence Central Schools

In a vote on 27 June 1946, Union Free School District No. 1 (Clarence, Lancaster and Newstead), Union Free School District No. 2 (Harris Hill) and many of the smaller one-room schoolhouses were centralized. New York State recognized the new district as the "Clarence Central School District," with Archie Harkness as the first Superintendent of Schools. Parker High School was deemed too small, and after much debate, the District purchased forty acres of land on the southeast corner of Main Street and Gunnville Road for a new high school.

Clarence Central High School

On 18 May 1948, the Clarence Central School District Board of Education called a meeting in the Parker High School auditorium to discuss construction of a new Junior-Senior High School. The total district enrollment was 1,200 students with 445 of them in grades 7 through 12. A site for the new school was not easily agreed upon as many residents preferred a location at Goodrich and Greiner Roads. They were afraid of the high traffic volume on Main Street. Interestingly, the board of education wrestled with many of the same fiscal issues that influence school budgets today. The official proposal promised to meet all needs without "frills." In the end, the new school at Main Street and Gunnville Road was dedicated on 4 May 1952.

17

Carroll Brothers Quarry

As railroads made their way through Clarence, there was a great demand for gravel to be used as ballast along the tracks. The Carroll family opened a gravel pit on the north side of Main Street, near Gunnville Road, to fulfill this need. The location of the stone crusher pictured below is visible on the map on page 11.

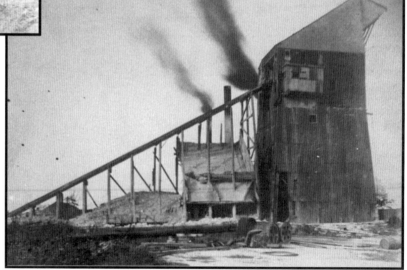

Accidents and fatalities were not uncommon. In 1909, John Bobald, a Hungarian immigrant, was killed after setting off an explosion. In 1919, the blasting in the pit opened a vein of water in the limestone and literally flooded the pit overnight. Much of the mining equipment, including a small locomotive engine, like the one pictured above, was left in the bottom of the lake that filled the quarry.

Many of the workers lived off Main Street near the quarry in an area called "Pumpkinville." It got its nickname from the extra orange paint the company gave to the workers to paint their houses.

Spaulding Lake

Elbridge Gerry Spaulding, grandson of former Buffalo Mayor and Congressman Elbridge Gerry Spaulding, was the founder of Spaulding and Yates which was, for a time, the largest wholesaler and retailer of coal in Buffalo. He settled in Clarence near the lake that had filled the Carroll Brothers Quarry. In December 1982, the Clarence Town Board approved the first phase of residential development around Spaulding Lake.

Strickler Meeting House

Ulrich Strickler led one of several Mennonite families that moved into Clarence in the early 1800's. In 1816, he purchased a plot of land at the northwest corner of Main Street and Strickler Road. In the 1810's, a log meeting house was built, but by 1825 it had fallen into disuse and was eventually replaced by the stone meeting house pictured above. Ulrich Strickler's son, John, was born in 1803. A farmer by trade, he was widely known throughout the Mennonite community as "a lay exhorter and spoke where there was opportunity."

Muchow Florist

Edward Muchow began his floral business when he was just nineteen years old. The original greenhouses, pictured above, were on the west side of Shisler Road on land he purchased from the Hamlin Estate. In 1914, the greenhouses were destroyed by fire. In 1922, he relocated to Salt Road just north of the West Shore tracks. In addition to floral arrangements, they also sold, "Rose Bushes, Shrubs, Hedges, Perennials, Tulips, Hyacinths, and Daffodil Bulbs." Their advertising slogan was, "Flowers for All Occasions...They Succeed Where Words Fail."

Wiltse Homestead

Livingston G. Wiltse was born in Clarence in 1817. His homestead was on Main Street almost opposite the Lusk Farm. Mr. Wiltse was a farmer for the first twenty-seven years of his life, but he also acquired a sound education and spent time teaching school in Clarence. He served seven terms as town supervisor and five terms as justice. His wife, Laura, was active in the Clarence Women's Christian Temperance Union in the 1880's. Livingston G. Wiltse passed away in 1900.

William Lusk Farm

In 1870, William Lusk and his wife, Levinia, purchased a ninety-five acre farm, including millpond, from Wayne Dodge. Mrs. Lusk was a Clarence native and a member of the first graduating class of Parker Academy. In addition to the millpond, the property contained a grove of maple trees. After completion of the West Shore Railroad, the grove became an Assembly Ground similar to the one at the Chautauqua Institution. The grove's most prominent event was the 100th birthday celebration for Lavina Fillmore, wife of the Reverend Glezen Fillmore. In 1910, the farm was purchased by the Automobile Club of Buffalo, and then purchased by the Town of Clarence in 1957 to be used as a town park.

Automobile Club of Buffalo

Almost from its inception, the Automobile Club of Buffalo (ACB) had ties with the Town of Clarence. In 1909, the ACB held their annual "Gymkhana" at Muegel's Hotel on Transit Road in Swormville. The Gymkhana consisted of competitions such as driving up and down wooden platforms with a bucket of water on the floor of the car. The driver who spilled the least amount of water won. In the March 1910 edition of *The Buffalo Motorist*, the club officers announced a search for a "Country Club House." Two months later, they purchased seventy acres of land in Clarence for the sum of $10, 600 with construction to begin "as soon as practicable."

ASSEMBLY HALL.
THE AUTOMOBILE CLUB OF BUFFALO,
CLARENCE N.Y.

Automobile Club of Buffalo

The country clubhouse of the Automobile Club of Buffalo was dedicated in 1911. The building was designed by the firm of August Esenwein and James Johnson. One of Buffalo's preeminent architectural firms, they had created the Temple of Music for the Pan-American Exposition in 1901. Many of their buildings, like the Niagara-Mohawk Tower, are still intact. The clubhouse was designed in the "Arts and Crafts" style influenced by Frank Lloyd Wright, Gustav Stickley and Elbert Hubbard. Adorning the top of the main staircase was a grandfather clock crafted for the clubhouse by Buffalo furniture maker Charles Rohlfs.

Automobile Club of Buffalo

By the 1920's, the Automobile Club of Buffalo (ACB) had a membership of almost 10,000. The clubhouse was open to all club members as well as members of any other club affiliated with the American Automobile Association. The facilities included a large clubroom, dining rooms and kitchen on the ground floor. The second floor had smaller dining rooms, salons and overnight accommodations. The grounds included a pond stocked with 10,000 trout and gardens donated, and reputedly tended by George Urban Jr., the Western New York milling magnate. The ACB sold the property to the Town of Clarence in 1957.

Clarence Historical Society Building

The Clarence Historical Museum is located on land that was originally part of a 144-acre purchase made by Asa Ransom in 1803. The land was purchased by the trustees of the First Society of Disciples of Christ in 1850. The congregation used local Onondaga limestone from "the Ledge" to construct a church. In 1875, the congregation sold the land to Dr. Jared Parker. When the Automobile Club of Buffalo acquired the William Lusk Farm, the building was purchased as a house for the groundskeeper. During the 1970's and 1980's it housed a series of restaurants including The Meeting House. In 1989, the Eleanor and Wilson Greatbatch Foundation purchased the land and building to be used for an historical museum, and in 1994 it was acquired by the Town of Clarence.

27

Abraham Shope House

Built on land originally belonging to Asa Ransom, the Shope House, located on the north side of the West Hill, was built by Pascal Pratt, a well-known Buffalo banker. Abraham Shope moved to the Hollow in 1800 with his parents but fled to Canada during the War of 1812. In the early 1840's, he bought the house from Mr. Pratt. In 1844, Abraham Shope gave a parcel of land on the south side of Main Street to the congregation of the Clarence Church of Christ.

Asa Ransom House Restaurant

The Asa Ransom House Country Inn stands on land first purchased by Asa Ransom. About 1803, he built the first grist mill in Erie County. The current building was constructed in 1853 and is "about thirty-five yards north of the old grist mill's remains." Prior to becoming a restaurant, the house belonged to Reuben Ebersole, who ran a store at the corner of Bank and Main Streets. The Zimmerman's operated it for a number of years as the Millroad Restaurant, a reference to the property's earlier use. The Asa Ransom House Country Inn opened in 1975 with some additions to the original Italianate structure.

Ebersole Mill

At the urging of Joseph Ellicott, Asa Ransom built a grist mill between 1804-1805. The power was provided by a creek flowing through the southern part of his property. Due to the relatively weak flow in Ransom Creek, the mill fell out of use in the 1830's. In 1842, Abraham Shope purchased the land, expanded the mill and damned the creek to create a millpond. After passing through a number of hands, Levi D. Ebersole purchased and significantly improved the mill in 1896. In 1917, it was sold to Millard P. Ryley. The mill was destroyed by fire in the 1920's and never rebuilt. Its remains are south of Main Street behind the Asa Ransom House Country Inn.

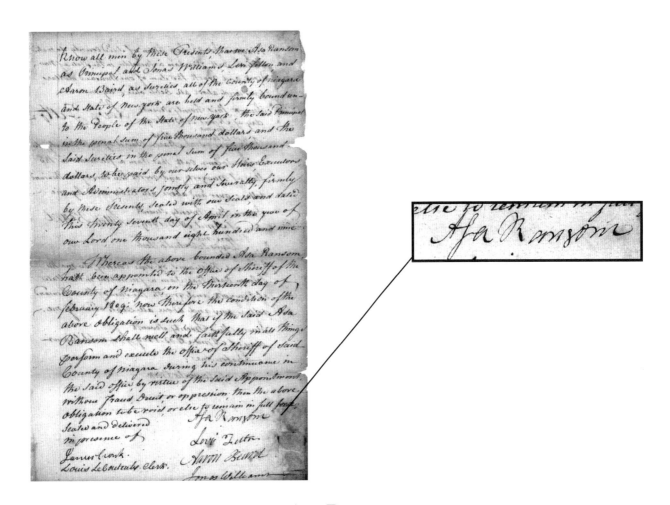

Asa Ransom

After serving in the American Revolution, Asa Ransom moved to Geneva, NY with his wife, Kezia. In 1799, he took advantage of an "offer of terms" and opened a tavern in Township 12, Range 6 of the Holland Land Purchase. The fledgling settlement was alternately known as Ransomville, Ransom or Ransom's Grove. In 1801, Joseph Ellicott moved his offices into the Ransom Tavern. In 1803, Ransom accepted a loan from the Holland Land Company to build a grist mill along the creek. Eventually, the mill was purchased by Levi D. Ebersole. The foundation still stands along Ransom Creek.

Asa Ransom

Incorporated 11 March 1808, Clarence originally encompassed most of northern Erie County. By 1833, the surrounding towns, as well as Buffalo, had been created, and the borders of Clarence looked very much as they do today. The descendants of Asa Ransom remained active in Clarence and Western New York after his death in 1835. His daughter, Sophia, is widely considered the first non-native born in New Amsterdam (Buffalo). His son, Asa, Jr., moved to Grand Island. Harry Bolton Ransom, considered the first male child born in Erie County, was active in the Church of Christ in the Hollow. Harry Bolton Ransom is pictured here, along with the falls near the Ransom sawmill.

Reverend Glezen Fillmore

The Reverend Glezen Fillmore was born in Bennington, Vermont in 1789. He came to Clarence on foot in 1809 to minister to both the educational and spiritual needs of the town. He married Lavina (sometimes spelled Lovina) Attwell, and they built their first house in Harris Hill. In 1813, they built a house, pictured above, on Ransom Road. A circuit minister for the Methodist Church, he often preached four full services in a day. Eventually, he oversaw a district that stretched from Lake Ontario to Meadville, Pennsylvania. Perhaps his most famous sermon was given in Buffalo at the hanging of the Thayer Brothers in 1825.

Lavina Fillmore

Although the Reverend Glezen Fillmore died in 1875, his wife, Lavina, lived another eighteen years. Born in Connecticut, she moved with her family to New Hartford in Oneida County, NY. After marrying Glezen Fillmore, cousin to Millard Fillmore, the 13th President of the United States, they first settled in Harris Hill. Owing to the great distances that her husband traveled, she remained on the Ransom Road farm and oversaw its sixty acres. Her 100th birthday was celebrated at Lusk Grove and was a major town event. She lived to be 106 years old. She and the Reverend Fillmore are buried in the Fillmore Cemetery, which seems appropriate since they donated the land upon which it was created.

Fillmore Cemetery

On 16 July 1863, the Reverend Glezen Fillmore was granted title to Lot #8 in Clarence. It was on this site, on the west side of Ransom Road, that he and his wife, Lavina, built their farm. On 16 June 1851, the Fillmores donated part of their land to create a cemetery. In 1864, the Methodist Church organized a cemetery association, and in light of the contribution of Reverend and Mrs. Fillmore, it was named the "Fillmore Cemetery." Over the next several years, the Fillmores donated close to two additional acres of land.

Castle Hill Farm

Peter Buechi purchased the farm that he called "Castle Hill" in 1892 from Lyman Parker. The land dates back to Lots #6 and #8 of the Holland Land Purchase. Those lots had originally been owned by the Reverend Glezen Fillmore. The 177-acre farm was renowned for its pears. The farm also boasted wind-driven pumps to provide its water needs. In 1917, the property was purchased by Millard P. Ryley, an executive with the Globe Elevator Company. Today, the Brothers of Mercy facility encompasses most of the old farm property. Ground was broken for the Brothers of Mercy Home in 1951.

Humbert's Store

In 1901, after graduating from the University of Buffalo with a degree in pharmacology, Arthur Humbert opened a store at the southwest corner of Main Street and Ransom Road on the site of the former J.B. Bailey Store. The Humbert Store sold assorted sundries, groceries and medicines. In 1920, he was forced to move his operation to the north side of Main Street when his property was purchased by Millard P. Ryley. After a summer of construction, Mr. Humbert opened his new store in the fall of 1920.

Hotel Claryle

In 1920, Millard P. Ryley bought the Humbert Store at the southwest corner of Main Street and Ransom Road. In order to clear the site to build the Hotel Claryle, he moved the store to a location back on Ransom Road where it was destroyed by fire in 1921. The hotel was open from 1921 to 1945 and featured guest rooms, a movie house, dance hall, drug store and ice cream parlor. In the 1950's, the building was the home of the Clarence Lumber and Supply Company. The building was destroyed by fire in the early 1970's.

Clarence Classical School

The first school in Clarence was located in the Hollow not too far from Asa Ransom's Tavern, and Rebecca Hamlin was the first schoolmistress. Having moved to Clarence in 1805, the Hamlins were among the first settlers in Clarence. In 1841, Mr. Hadley and Mr. Blennerhasset opened the Clarence Classical School on Main Street. When the school relocated to the top of Academy Street in 1852, the property was converted into a store, and in the early 1900's, it was remodeled to accommodate Wagner's Bakery, as pictured above.

The Bank of Clarence

The Bank of Clarence opened on 28 August 1920. The president of the bank was Millard P. Ryley who was also the founder of the Buffalo Truck and Tractor Company and owner of the Hotel Claryle. Ryley's farm was on Ransom Road just south of the Fillmore Cemetery. He owned various pieces of land in and around the Hollow. In the 1920's he was instrumental in bringing electricity to Clarence. During the Great Depression, the Bank of Clarence closed during President Roosevelt's mandated "Bank Holiday" but was one of the first local banks to reopen on 16 March 1933. The Bank of Clarence merged with M & T Bank in the late 1950's.

Kress Hotel

There has long been a hostelry at the corner of Main Street and Sawmill Road. Built in 1878, by George Kress, the building was long known as the Kress Hotel. For a brief time, it was the Hoffman House but then was sold to C.R. Cockle. By the 1920's, the building had been sold again and was then known as Ryan's Hotel. At the turn of the 20th Century, most residents knew it as the Valley Inn.

Wilson Greatbatch

Wilson Greatbatch, or Dr. Greatbatch, as many town residents call him, was born in Buffalo in 1919. Even in his youth, he showed a great affinity for electronics, first building his own shortwave radio and then joining the Sea Scout Radio Division. During World War II, "Bill" Greatbatch served as a radio operator and then as a rear gunner in torpedo and dive-bombers off the aircraft carrier *USS Monterey*. After the war, Mr. Greatbatch returned to Buffalo with his wife, Eleanor, and attended Cornell University on the GI Bill. After receiving his degree in electrical engineering, he went to work for Cornell Aeronautical Laboratory in Buffalo.

Wilson Greatbatch

In the mid-1950's, Mr. Greatbatch began to contemplate the idea of an implantable pacemaker. In 1958, Mr. Greatbatch first tested an experimental design in canines, with human clinical trials beginning in 1960. In the 1970's, Wilson Greatbatch, Ltd. was founded in Clarence to produce batteries designed to power the implantable pacemaker. Today, a division of Wilson Greatbatch Industries provides batteries for NASA. For his work, Mr. Greatbatch has received numerous awards and citations. In 1995, he told *Spectrum* magazine that his favorite award was being inducted into the National Inventor's Hall of Fame. On 16 June 1995, the workshop where he invented the pacemaker became the centerpiece of the Clarence Historical Museum's Industrial Heritage Wing.

The Schurr Sawmill

Located at the top of Sawmill Road, William Schurr operated a sawmill in approximately the same location as Asa Ransom's sawmill. He bought the land from Samuel Hummel in 1893. Eventually Mr. Schurr and his sons expanded to include cider milling and feed grinding. The mill could produce 5,000 feet of lumber per day, and in 1896 the cider mill produced 900 gallons of cider in five hours. The mill was one of the first businesses in Clarence to be electrified. The mill buildings were destroyed by fire in the 1930's. In its time, the Schurr house, Oakland Heights, was considered one of the most picturesque in the Hollow.

The Masonic Club

The Clarence Masonic Lodge was chartered on 6 March 1823 and has a long history in Clarence. From 1925 to 1926, the Masons built their clubhouse on Sawmill Road north of Stage Road with monies raised from dances. The two-acre site also included a picnic area, playground and baseball diamond. Herbert N. Rothenmeyer was the club's first president. In the 1960's, the club, along with students from Clarence High School, ran summer programs for children with special needs. The Clarence Masonic Club disbanded in 1974.

Clarence Methodist Church

In 1817, Clarence became an independent circuit of the Methodist Church and was served by the Reverend Glezen Fillmore. On 3 July 1833, the citizens of the Hollow organized the First Methodist Episcopal Church of Clarence. In 1872, the church and parsonage (visible on the left in the picture above) were destroyed by fire. Indicative of small town esprit, the Presbyterians invited the Methodists to worship in their building on Sunday afternoons. A new building was dedicated in 1874 with the dedicatory sermon preached by the Reverend Glezen Fillmore who died the following January. The church was torn down in 1962, and a new church was built at the southwest corner of Strickler and Greiner Roads.

The Clarence Church of Christ

The First Church of Christ was organized in Clarence in 1834. Initially, members met in homes, but in 1844 Abraham Shope gave the congregation a piece of land on the south side of Main Street at the top of the West Hill for a church. That original church building eventually passed into the hands of the Automobile Club of Buffalo and today houses the Museum of the Historical Society of the Town of Clarence.

In 1876, the congregation moved into this building at the foot of Sawmill Road.

The Dr. Henry Lapp House & Office

The son of Bishop John Lapp, Dr. Henry Lapp practiced medicine in Clarence for over fifty years. After graduating from the University of Buffalo, he opened his office on Main Street east of Ransom Road with the office adjacent to his residence. Over the years, the office changed orientation. In the picture to the left, the Italianate arches and bracketed eves faced west along Main Street. Dr. Lapp's house was completed in 1880.

The office was moved in 1883 to accommodate the West Shore Railroad.

In the picture above, the office has been turned to face Main Street. In 1916, Doctor Albert Erb purchased Dr. Lapp's house and had it moved to Sawmill Road where the top of the tower was removed. The house, pictured to the left, was lifted and moved intact. The office was moved across Main Street to become the office of his son Dr. Henry C. Lapp. This picture shows the house during its move. Dr. Erb, wearing a dark suit, is visble to the right of the workmen.

Peter Long Residence

Peter Long and his wife, Mary, lived near the Rothenmeyer residence on Main Street. "Postcard" Peter Long was an avid photographer and many of the images in this book are his. Among his other avocations, he served as a postal carrier for the Clarence Post Office. The mail route encompassed the area from East Clarence (Salt Road and the "Peanut Line") to Looneyville. In the 1850's, there was a brickyard located somewhere near his property. Like the Eshelman kiln in Clarence Center, many of the buildings in the Hollow were made from bricks fired locally. Peter Long died in 1947.

Klicker Funeral Home

Before entering the funerary business, Jacob C. Klicker had many occupations ranging from blacksmithing to barbering to running a stagecoach to Looneyville. By 1890, he opened an undertaking business on Main Street. The average cost of a funeral (casket, hearse and services) was $65. Jacob C. Klicker died in 1894. Eventually, Dr. Albert Erb moved his offices into the Klicker Building. When Bank Street was created, part of the Klicker Building was moved to the east side of Bank Street just north of Main Street.

The Rothenmeyer House

Born 11 January 1873, the younger Dr. Lapp was a graduate of Parker Academy. After attending medical school in Vermont, Dr. Henry C. Lapp returned to practice medicine in Clarence with his father. Eventually, he moved to Tonawanda, and in 1915, the house became the residence of the Rothenmeyers. His father's original doctor's office, to the right of the house, was moved north across Main Street. The Rothenmeyer Hardware Store was built on the site of the office in 1916.

J.H. & H.N. Rothenmeyer Coal and Hardware

John Rothenmeyer and his son, Herbert, went into business together in 1913. Their store sold a wide variety of items ranging from coal to fertilizer to farm tools. In 1916, they opened their store on the site of Dr. Lapp's old office. The store also served as a post office for a time with Herbert Rothenmeyer serving as postmaster for eighteen years. His son Herbert "Bill" Rothenmeyer took over the business after serving in the Army during World War II.

Parker-Havens Store

Although born in Newstead, Charles Parker was educated at Parker Academy. He settled in Clarence and was a farmer for a time. In 1892, he was appointed postmaster of Clarence and opened the post office in his hardware store. Upon his death in 1909, his wife, Mary, became postmistress. Charles Havens assisted Mrs. Parker with the store and eventually took over the business. In 1925, Hentcy's Restaurant opened in the old store. In the 1940's, Francis Shepard moved a dry cleaning business and funeral home into the Parker-Havens building. Even today, the building is immediately recognizable by the external staircase.

Bernhard House

It is likely that Levi Felton opened a hotel in this area as early as 1807. Over the years, several other proprietors ran inns on this site, but one of the best known was Bernhard House. In 1877, Peter Bernhard bought the building from Charles Bicker. In the 1920's, it was known throughout the Hollow as the Clarence Inn. After World War II, it went through yet another change. Veterans George Donovan and Melvin Ruszaj opened the Clarence Pharmacy in 1950. The post office was also relocated into the building. The pharmacy was torn down in the1970's.

James Guise Blacksmith Shop

John Guise may have opened a blacksmith shop as early as 1829. His son, James followed him into the trade. The original shop was located on the south side of Main Street near Ransom Creek. Eventually, James Guise built a brick shop along Main Street, west of the Presbyterian Church. His workbench is in the Clarence Historical Museum. It is unclear when the blacksmith shop went out of business. From contemporary accounts, it was still operating when the West Shore Railroad began service in the 1880's, but by the early 1900's, it was no longer in business.

Clarence Bowling Academy

By 1921, Ernie Udall's Garage, later the Clarence Garage, occupied the old James Guise blacksmith shop alongside the West Shore Railroad. Eventually, the Highway Department used the facility for storage before moving into the abandoned Liberty Diner factory on Salt Road. By the mid-1990's, the venerable building had found a new calling and became home to the Clarence Bowling Academy. The eight lanes have undergone several upgrades but probably none as significant as the last run of the West Shore.

The West Shore Line

Westbound, a West Shore locomotive crosses Main Street about 1896. The New York, West Shore and Buffalo Railroad was created in 1882, but the owners never expected it to be a successful business. Instead, they knew that rail baron Chauncey Depew did not like competition with his New York Central Railroad; they expected that Depew would purchase the West Shore just as he had done with his other competitors. After only a year of operation, the West Shore Railroad was bankrupt, and as expected, Depew then added the West Shore to the New York Central. Construction in the Hollow took place between 1882 and 1883, and the first train crossed Main Street on 1 January 1884. The steeple of the First Presbyterian Church is visible in the background, and the James Guise blacksmith shop is on the left.

Butler's Store

Roy Butler leased his ice cream parlor from George Gutekunst. Residents of the town remember that Butler's proximity to the school may have been convenient for him, but the high school principals had to make regular "sweeps" through the ice cream shop to keep students from being late for class. Parker's principals were not the only ones to worry about their students frequenting Butler's. Eddie King, the basketball and baseball coach often stopped by Butler's to make sure "that his school athletes weren't keeping late hours or overeating of Mr. Butler's milk shakes." In his later years, Roy Butler also served as the custodian at Parker Elementary.

Hummels' Store

Clara "Ma" Hummel and her husband, William "Doc" Hummel, ran a business at Main and Academy Streets. It is difficult to classify their establishment since they handled so many things. "Doc" was a barber; the store sold tobacco and penny candy, and they also ran the first garage and gas station in town. "Ma" Hummel recalled, "At one time we had eight different gas companies represented out front." "Doc" founded the store in 1909, but when he passed away in 1946, the store became know as "Ma" Hummel's General Store. She ran the store until 1960 and passed away in 1969.

Clarence Fire Department

The Clarence Fire Company dates its origin to March 1916. The fire department bought land on the west side of Academy Street for a fire hall, with their first equipment being a chemical pumper. Approved by the Town Board in 1922, the Clarence Fire Department became District No. 1 and was fully supported through taxes. The first Clarence fire truck, purchased in 1922, was assembled on the chassis of a "Buffalo Truck." A new fire hall was built on Bodine Road in 1955, and the current Clarence District No. 1 Fire Hall on Main Street was opened in 1973.

Clarence Academy

Built between 1850 and 1852, the Clarence Academy replaced the Clarence Classical School. The school cost $6,000 and was built on land donated by Dr. Jared Parker (inset). He also seeded a $15,000 endowment for the school with the condition that the town match the funds. In 1897, the north facade was added to the original building. By 1922, facilities at the Parker Academy were getting crowded, and an annex had been added. The town decided that the only real course of action was to build a new high school on the east side of Academy Street.

Parker High School

Parker High School was built on the southeast corner of the school park. It was designed as a three-story building that could accommodate 400 students. A gymnasium in the center of the building also served as theatre and concert hall. There were laboratories on the first floor, including one for "homemaking." The second floor housed classrooms as well as lockers and locker rooms. The third floor held a large room for study hall, offices for the administration and additional lab space. By 1936, enrollment had increased to a point where a wing was added to the southern portion of the building. After the Clarence Central School District built the high school on Main Street, Parker High was used as an elementary school.

Baseball Team sponsored
by the Gerber Sausage
Company

Parker Football Team
1909

Parker Girls' Basketball
1930

63

The Teachers' Training Class

In 1875, Parker Academy began offering courses for teacher training. The curriculum was generally the same as that of the students but according to Principal DeGroat, with the addition of "classes in theory and practice of teaching." When the building was expanded in 1897, the training classes were given their own area in the old part of the building. By that time, there was a more defined curriculum including school law, psychology and principles of education, civil government and subject reviews. There was also a state certification examination. The last training class, pictured above, graduated in 1931.

Burns Monumental Works

Charles Burns was born in Clarence on 16 October 1848 and educated locally. After his schooling was complete, he spent five years in Michigan before returning to Clarence to open the Burns Granite and Marble Works and Monuments. The workshop was located on Park Avenue near Parker High School. With the coming of the West Shore Railroad, work was made easier since stone could now be brought in by rail. When his son, Clarence, was old enough, the company became Burns and Son. Clarence Burns is standing in the middle of the photograph.

The Magoffin House

James Magoffin was born 22 March 1808, in Gettysburg, Pennsylvania and moved to Clarence in 1823, to pursue farming. He served as town supervisor in the 1870's. With the coming of the West Shore Railroad, the house was eventually occupied by Dan Wallis, the railroad stationmaster, and thus became known in the community as the "Railroad" house.

First Presbyterian Church of Clarence

The Presbytery of Niagara first met in 1817 on a lot given to them by the Holland Land Company. This ninety-acre grant lay in Newstead, which was not a problem when Newstead was part of Clarence. When Erie County was created and Newstead separated from Clarence, the Clarence members of the congregation chose the Hollow as their meeting place. In 1844, they erected their church at the corner of Main Street and Salt Road. The parsonage was on Ransom Road south of Main Street.

First Presbyterian Church of Clarence

In the 1950's, the congregation moved to a larger building on Main Street just east of Clarence High School. The property at Main Street and Salt Road was sold and became Landmark Furniture. In preparation for the changeover, the steeple was removed in November 1959. The second church in Clarence Hollow had "lost" its steeple. (See page 79)

Buffalo Truck and Tractor Company

The Buffalo Truck and Tractor Company was formed in 1917 with their production plant in the Hollow on Salt Road just north of Main Street. Due to World War I, production of the "Buffalo Truck" did not begin until 1921. Among its unique features was a dual transmission system. The advertising brochure noted: "On unpaved roads or ploughed fields, where hard, steady pulling is required, it can go as slow as one mile in six hours, or on the highway, it will attain a speed of 22 miles per hour." The company went bankrupt in 1924 having produced only about 150 vehicles. One of the last remaining Buffalo Trucks is on display at the Clarence Historical Museum.

THE NEW LIBERTY DINER
DESIGNED BY WARD

Liberty Diner Company

The Liberty Diner Company moved into the Buffalo Truck and Tractor factory in 1928. For the next three years, they were one of roughly fifteen Western New York companies to produce diner cars. The president of the company was Charles A. Ward. Ward had first worked with Lee Dickinson to manufacture the Ward & Dickinson diner cars in Silver Creek, NY. When that company incorporated, Ward left Silver Creek to begin Liberty Diner. The original Mazia's Pizzeria on the East Hill was a Liberty Diner.

R.A. Larkin Meats

Before becoming a meat market, this building had been a shoe store of some size. In 1888, William Loeffler purchased the property and converted it into a meat market. Richard Larkin was born in Clarence and graduated from Parker Academy in 1917. In 1923, he took over the corner shop and continued to operate it as a meat market. In the 1930's, the 8th Grade "Homemaking" classes from Parker High School went to Larkin Meats to study the different cuts of meat. Each student received a set of USDA meat charts. A set of these charts is on display at the Clarence Historical Museum.

Gutekunst Store

The Gutekunst store sits on property that can be traced all the way back to Joseph Ellicott in 1811. After the Civil War, it was briefly the site of a hotel and then later a store. One of the most well known owners was John C. Martin and his wife, Katherine, who villagers nicknamed "Auntie Martin." In 1920, George Gutekunst bought the building from Rudolph Henry. The Gutekunst store sold a variety of goods ranging from groceries to school supplies. In the 1950's the building housed an auto parts store.

West Shore House

Opened by William Spoor during the War of 1812, the West Shore House is one of the oldest buildings in town. Constructed out of native Onondaga limestone, it originally sported twelve fireplaces. Until 1870, it served as a stop on the stagecoach route between Buffalo and Batavia. During that time, three United States Presidents were registered guests: James Monroe, Millard Fillmore and Grover Cleveland. Unfortunately, the guest register, complete with Presidential signatures, was stolen in the 1950's.

Buffalo Road (Main Street)

Looking west from the East Hill, the West Shore House (also know as the Stone Hotel, Spoor's and the Tuttle Inn) is visible in the foreground. The First Presbyterian Church of Clarence and the Magoffin residence are visible on the right past Salt Road. The cupola of Dr. Lapp's House and the West Shore crossing are visible in the distance.

Buffalo Road (Main Street)

Looking east at the top of the East Hill in 1904, the German Reform Church is visible on the left. The goal of the roadwork was to cut down the steep descent of the East Hill. The logs were used to dampen the explosions set by the townsfolk working on the road. Pictured from left to right are:

Grace Bosworth (Long), Esther Carr (Gerber), Maud Bosworth (Humbert), Jennie Humbert and Stephen Gerber. Miss Utley is seated on the log to the right.

75

Odd Fellows' Hall

Clarence Lodge, No. 715, Independent Order of Odd Fellows (IOOF) was organized on 11 October 1894. By the early 1900's, the membership had grown to such an extent that they built a hall in Clarence. The cornerstone was laid on 20 May 1911 on land the IOOF had purchased from Dr. Henry C. Lapp. William Dietz did the carpentry, and Charles Burns did the stonework in the entry. In 1918, the Rebekah Lodge was chartered to "cultivate and extend the social and fraternal relations of life among Lodges and families of Odd Fellows." In 1952, a roller skating rink opened in the IOOF Hall.

Veterans

Clarence has connections to almost every military conflict that the United States has been engaged in. Pictured above are: (top left) Elizabeth "Betty" Smolka, a nurse in the United States Army Air Corps, in Gulfport, MS in 1944; (top right) Rollin "Rollie" Miller, in the Ordinance Division of the United States Army, in Luzon, Philippines in 1945; (bottom left) Norman Symington aboard *USS Harwood* in the Pacific Theatre of Operations during the Second World War; (bottom right) Clarence Veterans of the Civil War at the 1923 Grand Army of the Republic reunion.

German Methodist Church

The German Methodist congregation met for the first time in 1857 in Fred Klopp's wagon shop. By 1876, the congregation was in need of a new building and a new church was built on the south side of Main Street at the top of the East Hill. Eventually, the church membership combined with the congregation of English Methodists from the Hollow, and the building was taken over by the Erie County Pomona Grange #33. The Grange moved into the building in 1908. This picture was taken during the 1904 construction on Main Street.

The German Reform Church

Founded in 1859, this was the second building to house the German Reform Church of Clarence. The steeple blew down on 19 January 1907 and was replaced with the one visible in the photo below. Ironically, it was not the only church in the Hollow to lose its steeple! (See page 68)

Looking westward, the German Reform Church stood on the north side of the East Hill. The IOOF Hall is visible in the background. The service in German was dropped in 1918 during the height of World War I since the congregation wanted no doubts as to their allegiance. The congregation disbanded in 1928, and the building was moved to Bodine Road.

In the Business.

From A. to Z.

AMMONIA.
BOOTS & SHOES.
CROCKERY.
DRY GOODS.
EXTRACTS.
FLOUR.
GLASSWARE.
HATS and CAPS.
INK.
JARS and JUGS.
KITCHENWARE.
LARD.
MOLASSES.
NOTIONS.
OILCLOTH.
PAINTS.
QUART JARS.
RUBBER GOODS.
SOAPS.
TOBACCO.
UNDERWEAR.
VINEGAR.
WALL PAPER.
YARN.
ZENOLEUM.
ETC. ETC.

Weinauge & Co.
"Everything Worth While."

Weinauge Store

Edmund Weinauge was born in Germany in 1844 and moved to Clarence with his family when he was seven. He opened his store in 1884. A true "general store," Weinauge's sold everything from groceries to shoes to household furnishings. In addition to their store on the East Hill, the Weinauges also opened a creamery that produced butter, which was distributed all over Western New York. Although Mr. Weinauge died in 1922, the firm remained in business under the direction of his sons, Edwin and Alvin, until it closed on 6 December 1934. It was reopened in 1957 by Art Meininger who bought the store from Keith Harroun, the last descendant of the Weinauge family to manage the store.

Fay Graves Store

The son of Webster Graves, Fay Graves originally went into business in the old Humbert Store south of the Hotel Claryle. He left Clarence for a time while he ran a business in Akron. After he returned, he opened a store and undertaking parlor at the top of the East Hill in November 1936. The store was a typical, "five and dime," with the undertaking portion in the back. In 1940, competition increased when Shepard's Funeral Home opened. His brother Justus, a veteran of World War I, died of influenza while serving with the Marines in 1918. The Graves house is located at 10928 Main Street.

The Clarence Free Library

By the early 1930's, Esther Gerber (nee Carr) saw the value of a library for the citizens of Clarence. The first circulating library opened on 30 March 1933 with 1,500 volumes that were loaned out of the back two rooms of the Adams-Gerber House. Most of the volumes were donated by citizens of Clarence and Buffalo. By December 1933, the library moved to the second floor of the Ryley Building at the corner of Bank and Main Streets. A new building was commissioned to house the library. Built at a cost of $9,992.66, the library opened on 5 June 1936. Today, the Genealogy Department of the Clarence Historical Society is housed in the "Gerber" Library.

Dietz Lumber Yard

William Dietz was born in Germany and had thirteen children, one of whom was William Dietz, Jr. He was born in Clarence on 2 March 1861 and later moved with his family to Newstead. After attending school in Akron, he began a career in carpentry. In 1888, William married Elizabeth Schurr, and in 1896, opened a lumber and contracting business at the corner of Main Street and Schurr Road. In 1923, he purchased land behind the school park from John Lapp. He then built the Dietz Subdivision between East and West Avenues and Ransom Creek as a housing development. William and Elizabeth Dietz are buried in the Fillmore Cemetery.

Doctor Stern's House

Doctor Joseph Stern and his wife, Leontina "Lelly" Stern, fled Nazi Germany in 1938. Seeking a community in need of a physician, they settled in Clarence. Throughout his thirty-nine years of service, Dr. Stern was known for making frequent house calls and even caught a ride on a snowplow during a blizzard to deliver a baby. In the early days of his practice, Mrs. Stern recalled that some patients could not pay, but "brought me a rabbit, or they brought us corn or they brought us something they had to give." The Sterns lived in the former Dietz house next to the lumber yard. William Dietz and his family are pictured on the steps.

The Adams-Gerber House

Clarence is endowed with several houses that are not really what they seem to be. The Adams-Gerber House is actually a conventional house wrapped around a log cabin. The original cabin was built around 1850 with the property being purchased by Benjamin Adams shortly thereafter. Esther Carr grew up next to the cabin, and when she married sausage baron Stephen Gerber, they purchased the cabin and had a house built around it. The original cabin roofline, fireplace, beams and logs are still visible inside the house.

Rice-Sinclair-Brace House

Although there are several remaining log cabins in Clarence, few have sparked as much interest as this two-story log structure. Built around 1810, there is speculation that this might have been Asa Ransom's tavern. The original tavern was described by Joseph Ellicott as "two stories high with a spacious passage through the middle..." Certainly, this description matches the interior of the house today, and John Conlin, one of Western New York's prominent architectural historians has speculated that perhaps Asa Ransom's tavern was disassembled and moved to the top of the East Hill.

Our Lady of Peace

By 1920, there were eighteen families in the Hollow attending St. Theresa's Catholic Church in Akron. In 1921, the new parish purchased a parcel of land on the north side of Main Street on the East Hill. The brick church opened on 22 October 1922 under the direction of the Reverend Father John Uriel from the Akron church. In 1932, the Reverend Father Edward Godfrey assumed control of the parish, and during his tenure, he oversaw a number of improvements including the addition of a rectory.

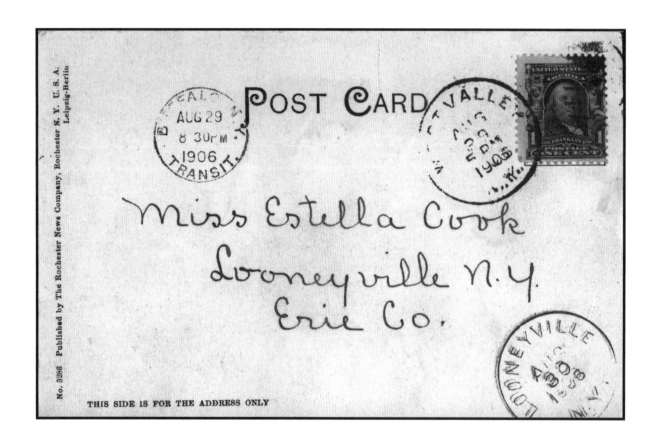

Looneyville

Located on the border of Lancaster, Alden and Clarence, Looneyville was a stop and post office on the New York Central Railroad. It seems to have been similar in nature to the stop on the West Shore Railroad at Gunnville. Although not immediately within the borders of Clarence, the post office served Clarence residents as evidenced by the postcard cancellation above. The stop got its name from Robert Looney who developed a lumber business selling timber to the railroad. The postcard is reproduced courtesy of Steve Merlihan whose relative lived on Klesat Road, now Northfield Road.

John Kraus Farm

John Kraus was born in Bowmansville in 1829 and moved to Clarence where he became famous for his agricultural innovations. In 1857, he began to experiment with varieties of wheat and in 1873 produced the first of a series of hybridized variations. The result was a higher yielding and hardier wheat. Due to his fame, Mr. Kraus served as town supervisor from 1875 to 1878; he was also the president of the Erie County Fair. He died in 1908. John Kraus and his wife, Christianna Bicksler, are pictured on the porch of the home, which is on the northeast corner of Greiner and Kraus Roads.

Forest View Dairy Farm

Paul Hoehman was born in Hamburg, NY in 1868. He moved to Clarence and opened Forest View Dairy Farm on Hoehman Road, now Greiner Road, just north of "the Ledge." The farm encompassed almost 141 acres, much of it used for the raising of Durham, Jersey and Holstein cattle. Other acreage was used for growing wheat, oats and fruit. He also maintained a sizeable stand of beech and maple trees. Naturally, the farm's specialty was dairy production, and the farm buildings included a creamery, icehouse and separator for making butter.

University of the State of New York

Examination Department

146TH EXAMINATION

NEW YORK STATE HISTORY

Wednesday, June 16, 1897 — 9:15 a. m. to 12:15 p. m., only

100 *credits, necessary to pass*, 75

Answer 10 questions but **no more.** *If more than 10 questions are answered only the first 10 of these answers will be considered. Each complete answer will receive 10 credits.*

1 Give an account of the first white settlement in New York, as to (*a*) the settlers, (*b*) the peculiar advantages of the place chosen, (*c*) the circumstances on which the settlers based their claims to the territory.

2 State and explain the attitude of the Iroquois toward the Dutch and English settlers and toward the French.

3 Show how the English first obtained possession of New York. What was the general condition of the colony at this time?

4 Give an account of the changes made in the government of the colony under Dongan, including (*a*) the assembly that was called to make a charter, (*b*) *three* provisions of the charter, (*c*) the permanent assembly provided for in the charter.

5 Give an account of the two parties that grew up after the execution of Leisler. Show how the political situation was affected by the coming of Governor Bellomont.

6 Describe the manner of raising money to meet public expenses of the colony under English rule. What was the principle concerning taxation for which the assembly contended and on what was this principle founded?

7 Give an account of the Zenger libel suit, covering (*a*) the circumstances leading to Zenger's arrest, (*b*) the organization of the Sons of liberty, (*c*) the trial of Zenger, (*d*) the significance of the result.

8 Write on *one* of the following topics relating to the time between the close of the French and Indian war and the outbreak of the revolution: (*a*) the making of new settlements toward the west and north, (*b*) Sir William Johnson and his land possessions.

9 The spirit of resistance was nowhere so strong as in New York. — *Bancroft*

Give facts to sustain this statement concerning the stamp act and other taxation acts of England.

10 What circumstances led to the organization of the Green Mountain boys? Describe the capture from the British of the forts at Ticonderoga and Crown Point.

11 Write on the following points concerning the Erie canal: (*a*) object of the canal, (*b*) reasons for the route selected, (*c*) what the canal has done for the state and for the west.

12 Give an account of *each* of the following: (*a*) part taken by New York state in the civil war, (*b*) draft riots in New York city.

13 Write on *three* of the following points concerning the public schools: (*a*) creation of the first permanent fund, (*b*) first state superintendent, (*c*) first free school act, (*d*) establishment of a permanent department of public instruction, (*e*) public schools made free, (*f*) compulsory education.

14 Give an account of *two* of the following events: (*a*) battle of Oriskany, (*b*) introduction of the steamboat, (*c*) the patriot war.

15 Write biographic notes on *five* of the following: Peter Stuyvesant, Corlaer, Isaac Jogues, Peter Schuyler, Stephen De Lancey, Philip Schuyler, Daniel Tompkins, Christopher Colles, Martin Van Buren.

Appendix B-Road Names

Academy Street-Parker Academy stood on the west side of Academy Street

Alexander Drive-The Barnums, owners of the Shope House, named the street after their son Alexander

Bank Street-Was created to connect Main Street and Greiner Road. The Bank of Clarence stood on the northwest corner

Gunnville Road-The Gunn family lived on Gunnville, south of the present high school

Howe Road-Doctor Howe lived on the east side of town near the Newstead line

Kraus Road-Named for John Kraus, farmer and former Town Supervisor

Bodine Road-The Bodine family lived just south of the Hollow

Ransom Road-Asa Ransom, the first settler in the Hollow

Salt Road-Residents hoped that salt from the Erie Canal would be transported down this road

Sawmill Road-The trail up to Asa Ransom's sawmill

Schurr Road- Gottleib Levi Schurr, related to the Long, Muchow and Dietz families

Shisler Road-John Shisler, owned Sunny Slope Dairy Farm

Strickler Road-John Strickler, owned a farm and preached at the church at Main Street and Strickler Road

Tillman Road-Used to be an old railroad bed

Appendix C-Architecture

Log Cabin

The log cabin is not native to North America. The design was first used by Swedish colonists in "New Sweden" (Delaware) in the early 1600's. The design was convenient for settlers on the frontier since it did not require "hardware" like iron nails. The ends of the logs were notched to hold them together and the spaces between them chinked with mud or moss and horse or pig hair.

Clarence has a number of extant log cabins. In the Hollow, the Brace House and Adams-Gerber House are log constructions. Although its original location was on Goodrich Road near Lapp Road, the Goodrich-Landow Cabin, built circa 1820, is now located next to the Clarence Historical Museum.

Federal

According to Austin Fox, the author of *Erie County's Architectural Legacy*, the Federal Style is one of the oldest architectural designs in Erie County. This design may also be referred to as Adam style. The West Shore House is an excellent example of this type of architecture, which was common until the 1830's. One of key design elements is the five-bay opening: two windows, a central door and two windows. Similar to the Brace House, many Federal style buildings had chimneys at both ends. Other common features, visible on the West Shore House, are the quarter-moon windows on the eastern and western ends of the building, and the fanlight over the entry door.

Greek Revival

Toward the end of the Federal period, Greek Revival architecture became widespread in Western New York. Architectural historians have made the connection between the temple styles of ancient Greece and the flourishing democracy in the fledgling United States. One of the key design elements is the triangular, temple-appearance. Clearly visible on the Schmidt House are the cornice returns and pilasters at the corners. The door is framed by pilasters and a lintel.

Italianate

Italianate design was embraced by an increasing upper class that had the disposable wealth to construct these elaborate homes. Many Italianate buildings have a cupola or tower. This element is a carry-over from houses built near the sea. One of the most common features is the eve brackets in single or double pairs. Also common were double or coffin doors that allowed for wakes to be held in the house. Visible here on the Magoffin House are rounded, segmented windows.

Victorian

In the later half of the 19th century, several architectural styles merged into what is commonly called "Victorian." Second Empire, Eastlake, Queen Anne and Stick styles are the most prevalent "Victorian" styles. The Rothenmeyer House is a Stick style dwelling. This type of house derives its name from the "stickwork" or patterns of boards raised from the wall surface. One of the characteristics of this period is the reproduction of Gothic design elements in wood rather than stone. This can be seen in the decorative truss below the front gable. The Rothenmeyer House also has a distinctive tower on the southwest corner.

American Foursquare

The American Foursquare was common in the United States and popular throughout Clarence. Four square rooms on the ground floor are linked by an interior stairway to four square rooms on the second floor. This design allowed for a large house to be built on a relatively small lot. The design became so popular that catalog retailers like Sears, Roebuck actually sold the Foursquare as a kit. All the pieces were pre-cut; it was then delivered by railroad and erected on site.

Arts and Crafts

The Arts and Crafts style began in England in the early 1900's but was given a uniquely American twist by craftsmen like Frank Lloyd Wright, Charles and Henry Greene and Elbert Hubbard. Drawing their influence from nature, the designs are integrated in the popular "bungalow." The bungalow design is quickly recognizable by the large front porch supported by piers, visible rafter tails and braces and a protruding dormer.

Street   Index

Many   buildings   in   this   book   are   still   standing.   See   the   index   below   for   their   current   address

Bibliographic Notes:

Marshalling the sources for this book has been a fascinating experience. In many areas, we have abundant resources, and I have been aided by numerous people who provided the perfect documents at the right time. There are, however, areas where primary sources are scattered or virtually non-existent. For instance, we have some documents with Asa Ransom's signature, but no journals or letters. In cases like this, I have drawn upon the oldest available secondary sources. The two that seem to form the bedrock of Clarence history are the 1876 *Centennial History of Erie County, New York* and the 1924 *History of Clarence: Past and Present*. In my opinion there was still a chance of "first-person" recollection. I have tried to be meticulous in the bibliography that follows. One final note, many dates vary by a year or two depending on the available sources. I have done my utmost to try to establish a commonality among the dates, but that was not always possible, and so, in some cases, I have referred to a period rather than a specific year.

Primary Source Note:

The photographs in this volume are the property of the Historical Society of the Town of Clarence, except where noted.

The following folios are in the collection of the Genealogy Department of the Historical Society of the Town of Clarence housed in the Gerber Library:

File 85-25: Fillmore Diaries

File 80-15-C: Memorial of Rev. Glezen Fillmore, D.D.

Asa Ransom House
Auto Club
Automobile Club
Bank of Clarence
Beeman
Clarence Bowling Academy
Clarence Fire Department
Clarence High School Proposed Site
Clarence Historical District
Clarence Methodist Church
Fillmore, Glezen
German Reformed Church
Greatbatch
Holland Land Company
Kraus, John
Long, Peter
Lusk
Lelly Stern: In Her Own Words (DVD)
Looneyville
Masonic Club
Muchow, E.A.
Morlando: The Harris Hill Gardens
Ransom, Asa
Road Books
Rohlfs

Rothenmeyer
Shurr
Schurr/Dietz
Strickler
"Early History of the Clarence Fire Department,"
Glen C. Burns
Volume "FH" of Clarence Families
Volume "ST" of Clarence Families
Weinauge
West Shore House
West Shore Railroad

The following folios are in the collection of the
Historical Society of the Town of Clarence housed
in the Historical Society Museum:

Asa Ransom Sheriff's Bond-original letter
History of the Clarence Historical Society Museum
(compiled by Julie Warham)

The following folios are in the collection of the
Clarence Town Historian housed at the Clarence
Town Park Clubhouse:
Arthur Humbert
Blacksmiths
Clarence Businesses

Clarence Fire Department
Gerber-Adams House
Schurr Sawmill

Files on the history of the Clarence Central School
District, housed in the District Central Offices.

Interviews
David Brace (23 July 2002)
Robert Buyers (26 July 2004)
Sue Dietz (8 December 2004)
Lawrence Haberer (7 August 2004)
Viola Monkelbaan (12 January 2005)
Betty Smolka (26 July 2004)
Betty Smolka (8 December 2004)

Webpages
"American Foursquare Floor Plans,"
http://architecture.about.com/library/bl-foursquare-
sears-chelsea.htm

'Bogalusa Story by C.W.Goodyear,"
http://freepages.genealogy.rootsweb.com/
~mcclendon/Bogalusa/Bogalusa%20Story/
eBook%20-%20Bogalusa%20Story/

PPC%20version%20-%2072%20dpi%20-%20smaller/BogalusaStory-with-photos-PPC.html

"Buffalo as an Architectural Museum," http://ah.bfn.org/a/bamname.html

"Buffalo in1797," http://www.buffalonian.com/history/articles/%3c1800/Buff1797.html

"Buffalo in 1799 Settlement Spreads," http://www.buffalonian.com/history/articles/%3c1800/Buff1799.html

"Lockport's Gulf Wilderness Park," http://www.lockport-ny.com/Tourism/Parks3.htm

"Onondaga Limestone," http://www.preservationcoalition.org/bam/vocab/mat/onan

"Short Course : The UCC and German Reformed Church," http://www.ucc.org/aboutus/shortcourse/reformed.htm

'Ward & Dickinson Dining Car Company," http://www.geocities.com/cornwallace55/wdmain.html

"Wilson Greatbatch-Inventor of the Pacemaker is 75," http://www.biophan.com/news2_011802-2.php

Articles

Brace, Doris, "The Old Log Cabin Stage Coach Stop, " *The Clarence Press*, August, 1944.

Conlin, John, "The Early Log Architecture of Western New York,"*Western New York Heritage*, Winter, 2003.

Conlin, John, "The Goodrich-Landow Cabin: A Document of Pioneer History," *Western New York Heritage*, Summer 2004.

Rising, Gerry, "Sinking homes were built on an cient wetlands," *Buffalo News*, 26 June 2004.

Sentz, Lynda Wade, "Discovery Adds to History: Ransom's Tavern May Have Been Located," *Clarence Bee*, 5 March 1997.

Stoddard-Schofield, Nikki, "Mennonites And Related Groups of Clarence, Erie County, New York, In the Nineteenth Century." *Pennsylvania Mennonite Heritage*, July 1983.

Published Sources

Annual Garden Tour Clarence Center Community Association, July, 2004.

Baker, Oneta. *History of the Town of Clarence.* Interlaken: Heart of the Lakes Publishing, 1983.

Berton, Pierre. *Niagara:A History of the Falls.* Toronto: McClelland & Stewart, Inc., 1992.

Buffalo Motorist. A Publication of the Automobile Club of Buffalo, 1909.

Buffalo Motorist. A Publication of the Automobile Club of Buffalo, 1910.

Buffalo Motorist. A Publication of the Automobile Club of Buffalo, 1911.

Buffalo Motorist. A Publication of the Automobile Club of Buffalo, 1912.

Clarence: Sesquicentennial. Town of Clarence Sesquicentennial, Inc. 1958.

Cook, Laura Lincoln. *The War of 1812 on the Frontier.* Buffalo: Buffalo and Erie County Historical Society, 1961.

Conover, Jewel Helen. *Nineteenth-Century Houses in Western New York.* Albany: SUNY Albany Press, 1966.

Dunn, Edward. A History of Railroads in Western New York. Buffalo: Canisius College Press 2000.

Fox, Austin, ed. *Erie County's Architectural Legacy.* Erie County: The Erie County Preservation Board, 1983.

Grande, Joseph. *Images of America-Amherst.* Chicago: Arcadia, 2004.

Greatbatch, Wilson. *The Making of the Pacemaker: Celebrating a Lifesaving Invention*. Amherst, NY: Prometheus, 2000.

Isachsen, Y.W., *et.al. Geology of Western New York: A Simplified Account*. Albany: New York State Museum, 2000.

Illustrated Historical Atlas of Erie Co. New York from Actual Survey and Records. New York: F.W. Beers & Co., 1880.

Johnson, Crisfield. *Centennial History of Erie County, New York; Being its Annals from the Earliest Recorded Events to the Hundredth Year of American Independence*. Buffalo: Mathews & Warren, 1876.

McAlester, Viginia & Lee. *A Field Guide to American Houses*. New York: Alfred Knopf, 2004.

Merken, Alan, ed. *1927 Edition of the Sears, Roebuck Catalogue*. Crown Publishers, Inc., 1970.

Morgan, Lewis Henry. *League of the Iroquois*. New York: Corinth Books, 1962.

New Century Atlas, Erie County, New York. 1909.

Sears, Roebuck Catalog of Houses, 1926. New York: Dover Publications, Inc., 1991.

Smith, H. Perry, ed. *History of the City of Buffalo and Erie County with Illustrations and Biographical Sketches of Some of its Prominent Men and Pioneers*. Volume I. Syracuse: Smith and Bruce, 1884.

Silsby, Robert. *Settlement to Suburb: A History of the Town of Tonawanda Erie County New York, 1607-1986*. Tonawanda, NY: Sterling Sommer, Inc., 1997.

Silsby, Robert. *The Holland Land Company in Western New York*. Buffalo and Erie County Historical Society, 1961.

The History of Clarence: Past and Present. Issued by the Clarence Community Council, 4 July 1924.

Tuner O. *Pioneer History of the Holland Land Purchase of Western New York: Embracing Some Account of the Ancient Remains*. Buffalo: Jewett, Thompson & Co., 1850.

Wilner, Merton. *Niagara Frontier: A Narrative and Documentary History*. Clarke Publishing: Chicago, 1931.

White, Truman, ed. *Our County and its people: A Descriptive Work on Erie County New York, Vol.1*. The Boston History Company, 1898.

Index

Symington, Norman 77

T

Teachers' Training Class 64
Thayer Brothers 33
The Buffalo Motorist 24
The Ledge 15, 27, 90
Treaty of Big Tree 13
Tuttle Inn 74

U

University of Buffalo 37, 48
Urban Jr., George 26
Uriel, Father John 87
USS Harwood 77
USS Monterey 42

V

Valley Inn 41

W

Wagner's Bakery 39
Wallis, Dan 66
War of 1812 28, 73
Ward & Dickinson 70
Ward, Charles A. 70
Weinauge, Alvin 80
Weinauge, Edmund 80
Weinauge, Edwin 80
Weinauge Store 80
West Shore House 73, 74, 94
West Shore Railroad 15, 21, 23, 55, 56, 57, 65, 66, 74, 88
West Transit Line 14
William Lusk Farm 22, 23
Wilson Greatbatch, Ltd. 43
Wiltse Homestead 22
World War I 69, 79, 81

World War II 42, 52, 54, 77
Wright, Frank Lloyd 25

Douglas Kohler is a life-long resident of Clarence. A member of Clarence High School's class of 1984, he has degrees in history and education from Canisius College. He has taught 7th grade history at Clarence Middle School since 1989. He is actively involved with the Clarence Historical Society and the Town of Clarence Bicentennial Committee. He lives in Clarence Center with his wife, Charlotte, and his Siamese cat, Sebastian.